A Note to Parents

DK READERS is a compelling program for beginning readers, designed in conjunction with leading literacy experts, including Dr. Linda Gambrell, Professor of Education at Clemson University. Dr. Gambrell has served as President of the International Reading Association, National Reading Conference, and College Reading Association.

Beautiful illustrations and superb full-color photographs combine with engaging, easy-to-read stories and informational texts to offer a fresh approach to each subject in the series. Each DK READER is guaranteed to capture a child's interest while developing his or her reading skills, general knowledge, and love of reading.

The five levels of DK READERS are aimed at different reading abilities, enabling you to choose the books that are exactly right for your child:

Pre-level 1: Learning to read

Level 1: Beginning to read

Level 2: Beginning to read alone

Level 3: Reading alone

Level 4: Proficient readers

The "normal" age at which a child begins to read can be anywhere from three to eight years old. Adult participation through the lower levels is very helpful for providing encouragement, discussing storylines, and sounding out unfamiliar words.

No matter which level you select, you can be sure that you are helping your child learn to read, then read to learn!

LONDON, NEW YORK,
MELBOURNE, MUNICH, AND DELHI

Editor Victoria Taylor
Designer Owen Bennett
Senior Designer Lynne Moulding
Brand Manager Ron Stobbart
Art Director Lisa Lanzarini
Managing Editor Catherine Saunders
Publishing Manager Simon Beecroft
Category Publisher Alex Allan
Production Controller Clare McLean
Production Editor Siu Chan

Reading Consultant
Linda B. Gambrell, Ph.D.

First published in the United States in 2009
by DK Publishing
375 Hudson Street
New York, New York 10014

09 10 11 12 13 10 9 8 7 6 5 4 3 2
DD526—01/09

DK Books are available at special discounts when purchased in bulk
for sales promotions, premiums, fund-raising, or educational use.
For details, contact: DK Publishing Special Markets,
375 Hudson Street, New York, New York 10014
SpecialSales@dk.com

Published in Great Britain by Dorling Kindersley Limited.
A catalog record for this book is available from the Library of Congress.

ISBN: 978-0-7566-4510-6 (Paperback)
ISBN: 978-0-7566-4509-0 (Hardback)

Color reproduction by MDP
Printed and bound by L-Rex, China

Discover more at
www.dk.com
www.LEGO.com

On the Farm

Written by Victoria Taylor

This is a farmer.

He sometimes drives a tractor around the farm.

There are many
animals on the farm.
Come and meet them!

This is a cow.
Cows go 'moo'.

'Baa' says the sheep
on the hill.

This is a horse.
Horses go 'naay'.

This is a pig.
Pigs go 'oink'.

'Woof-woof' says
the farmer's dog.

This is a cat.
Cats go 'meow'.

'Cock-a-doodle-do'.
The hen wakes
everyone up.

Sometimes the farmer's children ride the horses. It's great fun!

The horses also have a cart that the children can ride in.

The children feed the horses carrots. Yum!

The horses can jump
over fences.
They have won a
trophy for jumping!

The farmer's family has a pet dog. He has spots on his coat.

They also have a pet cat. The cat likes to sit near the horses' stable.

There is a baby pig on
the farm. Baby pigs are
called piglets.

This piglet sometimes sits in the farmer's wheelbarrow.

This is the farm's helper.

He drives the combine
harvester. A combine
harvester is a machine
that cuts corn.

Combine harvesters make hay bales and drop them out of the back of the machine.

The hay bales need to be stored away.

The hay bales go up
a long conveyor belt
into the barn.

The farmer's wife helps to store them away.

The tractor can pull
a plow. The plow turns
soil over so it will be
ready for planting.

A roller can be fixed to the tractor. The roller flattens the soil so seeds can be planted.

There is always a lot to do on the farm.

Even the farm animals sometimes need a rest!

Picture Word List

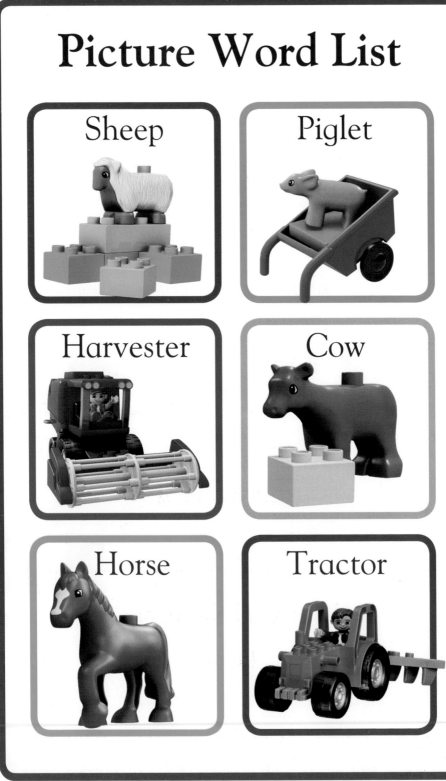

Sheep

Piglet

Harvester

Cow

Horse

Tractor